Atkins Thyroid Cure

Heal Your Metabolism Gland And Lose 45 lbs This Month

Sherry S. Williams

Atkins Thyroid Cure: Heal Your Metabolism Gland And Lose 45 lbs This Month

This book was self-published with the amazing help of <u>Self-Publishing Made Easy Now!</u> [1] . You can grab a free copy of the checklist that started my journey here: <u>FREE Self-Publishing Checklist</u> [2] .

[1] https://selfpublishingmadeeasynow.com/xpjv

[2] https://selfpublishingmadeeasynow.com/free_checklist

Table of Contents

1 - Introduction

Millions of people wish to lose weight, but many find it hard to do so. No matter how many diets they try, they can't seem to shed their excess weight. Health experts would advise that they see their doctors first to check if they have any underlying conditions before they start on any type of exercise or diet regime.

According to the American Thyroid Association, approximately 20 million people in America have a form of disease concerning their thyroid. The association also mentioned that more than 12% of their population has high chances of developing thyroid conditions, and up to 60% of those who have thyroid problems are unaware that they suffer from such.

Women are also more prone to develop thyroid problems compared to men. When thyroid problems or diseases are undiagnosed, these may increase the risk of developing more serious conditions, such as infertility, cardiovascular diseases, and osteoporosis.

By following the Atkins Thyroid Cure, the thyroid gland will be healed, and this will then help one's metabolism to be "fixed". The thyroid gland is a small gland, but it can influence the entire body.

What is the thyroid gland, and why is it important?

The thyroid is a small gland that can be found at the lower part of the neck. It produces a hormone that is responsible for regulating a person's metabolism. The metabolism is responsible for producing energy from oxygen and nutrients, and this has a direct effect on many important body functions like the heart rate and energy level.

There are certain conditions that could affect the thyroid gland, and it is important that people also watch out for these conditions. One such condition is hypothyroidism. It's a condition wherein the gland is not able to make enough of the thyroid hormone. Some of the symptoms that may manifest include depression, extreme feelings of tiredness, forgetfulness, and for many, weight gain.

Another condition is hyperthyroidism, which is a condition that causes the gland to make too much of the thyroid hormone. The symptoms of this include sleep disturbances, irritability, muscle weakness, vision problems, weight loss that is unexplained, and nervousness. Graves' disease is one type of hyperthyroidism.

With this information, it is important to keep track of one's thyroid health. The Atkins Thyroid Cure will help the thyroid to get back in shape, and in turn, affect the body's metabolism. This will then help people who wish to lose weight to do so in a faster way. The key is to have the thyroid tested if it is sluggish and is affecting the metabolism. Thyroid problems also serve as a gateway for other problems. Once the thyroid's health has been established, there are many ways of helping to correct and heal the thyroid.

2 - Getting Started

There are actually many reasons why the thyroid functions in stalled levels, but many patients and health professionals ignore this. There have been instances where a person had a body fat percentage of more than 30, but the number didn't go down even with vigorous physical activities. Even when paired with a good diet, the fat percentage wouldn't go down. There are also other accompanying symptoms, such as a depressed mood. There is a chance that this person is suffering from some sort of thyroid problem.

However, it takes more than just mere testing in order to check if the thyroid has problems. Correcting thyroid issues require an approach that is integrative in nature. It involves more than just taking a pill. It involves different aspects, such as elimination of certain types of food in the diet, nutritional support, reduction of stress and inflammation, exercise, and a lot more.

The diet plays a big role in treating and healing the thyroid gland. Recently, there have been reviews of people going on a low-carbohydrate diet, and they mention that it has helped them have smaller waistlines. There is also great evidence that shows how a low-carb diet can also help one's thyroid. Italian scientists have asked people who have sluggish thyroids to reduce their carbohydrate intake to the levels that Atkins Diet followers do. This test was done just recently.

The results that they gathered were the following:

- The test subjects were able to reduce 5% of their respective body weights in just a span of three weeks.

- There was also a 44% reduction in chemicals found in the blood that worsen or trigger thyroid disease.

They also did a test on another group, and this group was told to cut down on their calories instead of their carbohydrate intake. The result was a spike in the thyroid-harming compounds. It shows that going on a low-carbohydrate diet is a lot better than restricting calories.

By following the Atkins diet, the thyroid will be healthy. A healthier thyroid means that a person will also be able to lose weight easily and keep the excess pounds off. Many people are following the low-carb diet plan, and that is why they are sticking with the Atkins Diet.

Another clinical study that was published by the New England Journal of Medicine in 2008 found out that people who were on a low-carbohydrate diet were able to lose more weight than those who were on a low-fat diet. Those on low-carb diets also showed better levels of their blood lipids.

In 2013, a low-carbohydrate diet was also seen to be effective in helping people with diabetes improve their blood sugar level. This was according to a study conducted in 2013 and published in the Journal of the American College of Nutrition.

So how do you start the Atkins Thyroid Diet?

In order to achieve the closest results to the Italian study, the Atkins 40 plan is recommended. This plan allows a person to take in 40 grams of carbohydrates per day. As a rule, every main meal should have about 4-6 ounces of protein, up to 10 grams of carbohydrates, and one serving of fat. You can then have 10 grams of carbohydrates for your snacks.

There are many carbohydrate trackers that you can use, such as the free one at Atkins.com. This will help you to stay under your daily carbohydrate limit. In order to stay in optimal health, experts recommend that 15 grams of carbohydrate should be from vegetables.

Why does cutting carbohydrates make you thinner?

Scientists have known for a long time that the body changes carbohydrates into blood sugar. It then uses the converted sugar as its main source of fuel. However, when a person eats more carbohydrates than necessary, the body overproduces insulin, which is a hormone that promotes quicker storage of fat.

By restricting one's carbohydrate intake in the Atkins diet, the body is forced to stop using blood sugar as a main source of fuel. It resorts to burning fat for energy. As an added bonus, when the body burns fat as the main source of energy, ketones are released in the body. These are natural compounds that are produced from the burning of fat and they help to reduce one's hunger!

When you cut down on your carbohydrate intake, you are also revving your thyroid. A research conducted by the University of Michigan found that cutting calories means that you are also starving the thyroid. The thyroid is suppressed and cannot work as needed. When you are on Atkins, you are not cutting down on calories, which is why the thyroid is not stressed. The Italian scientists also found that by following a low-carbohydrate diet, the autoimmune attacks on the thyroid gland are reduced.

Autoimmune attacks are those instances when the body makes antibodies that attack and damage the thyroid. This is the most common cause of thyroid disease. The University of Maryland's study suggests that there are proteins found in grains that can trigger the body to create antibodies. Once you reduce your intake of grains in a low-carbohydrate diet, this can help to stop the problem, as said by Michael Ruscio, D.C., an expert on autoimmunity.

Dr. Ruscio makes it a routine to prescribe a diet that has reduced carbohydrate intake in order to protect the thyroid of his patients. He has seen impressive results among his patients. There have been weight loss reports of up to 45 pounds in a span of 30 days. There are also patients who reported that by following the Atkins Thyroid Diet, their symptoms related to sluggish thyroids have been relieved.

The secret to this diet is that it does not push a person to starve.

Other reports of people suffering from hypothyroidism becoming better have also surfaced everywhere. Women who have suffered from other problems, such as polycystic ovary syndrome (PCOS) who followed the Atkins Thyroid Diet have also found that their symptoms have diminished. Energy levels rose, pounds were shed, and overall, they felt better about themselves.

3 - Meals

When you are on the Atkins Thyroid Diet, it doesn't mean that you will settle with eating bland types of food. A lot of nutrition teams have gone out of their way to create Atkins 40 menus for people to try. When you are also on the Atkins Thyroid Diet, it is important that you also drink a lot of water.

You may also take other extras and beverages that contain little to almost no carbohydrates, such as tea, coffee, spices, vinegar, and certain zero-calorie sweeteners. It is best that you check with your doctor before you go with any plan.

Here is an example of meal options to follow when you are on the Atkins Thyroid Diet:

BREAKFAST

Option 1: 2-3 slices of bacon (cooked any style) plus 2 eggs, and an Atkins-friendly muffin (recipe below)

Option 2: 2 ounces of ham and an almond-raspberry smoothie (recipe below).

Atkins Muffin

- ¼ cup almond meal

- ¼ tsp. baking powder

- 1 tsp. sweetener (zero-calorie)

- ½ tsp. cinnamon

- pinch of salt

- 1 egg

- 1 tsp. coconut oil, melted

In a coffee mug, mix the almond meal, sweetener, baking powder, salt, and cinnamon. Then add in coconut oil and egg and mix until everything is well-combined. Put in the microwave for a minute.

Almond Raspberry Smoothie

- 4 ounces Greek yogurt

- 20 almonds

- ½ cup raspberries

- ½ cup almond milk (unsweetened)

In a blender, put everything together until well blended.

LUNCH AND DINNER

Option 1: 4 to 6 ounces of boiled shrimp or crab with butter (melted) and seafood "rice" (recipe below)

Option 2: 4 to 6 ounces of roast beef (with its juices), 10 roasted baby carrots with olive oil plus herbs, 1 cup of mushrooms, mixed greens (2 cups) with a dressing of choice that is zero-carbohydrate.

Option 3: 4 to 6 ounces of canned salmon or tuna, 1 teaspoon dill relish and one tablespoon mayonnaise, 1 cup raspberries, 1 cup sliced cucumber, zero-calorie sweetener (optional), and a drizzle of heavy cream.

Option 4: No Chop Chili (recipe to follow)

Option 5: 4 to 6 ounces of roasted chicken, ½ cup of guacamole, and 1 cup sliced bell pepper.

Seafood "Rice"

- 1 cup of cauliflower rice

- butter or olive oil

- ½ cup green peas

- Old Bay seasoning (a pinch)

Thaw the cauliflower rice and then pat dry using paper towels. Using olive oil or butter, sauté the rice and add the seasoning and ½ cup of green peas.

No Chop Chili

- 1 pound of ground meat

- 2 to 3 teaspoons of chili powder

- 1 cup of prepared salsa (mild)

- 1/3 cup of Cheddar cheese, shredded

- 1/3 cup of green bell pepper, chopped

- 2 tablespoons of sour cream

In a medium-sized pan, brown the meat and add in the chili powder. Stir the salsa in. Divide into 4 servings. You can then garnish with cheese, bell pepper, and sour cream.

For snacks, you can opt to eat vegetables with mayonnaise, pumpkin seeds or almonds, or beef jerky. To make the best out of the diet, make sure that about 15 grams of the total carbs you eat every day are from vegetables.

4 - Coping Methods

In order for this to work, you have to integrate a lot of elements to make the best and most successful set of methods to help you cope with thyroid issues. Here are some strategies that you may follow:

Take out the ones that cause problems of the thyroid.

It is important that you carefully consider anything that could interfere with the normal functions of your thyroid. When you have done so, eliminate these things. There are actually many things that could inhibit the proper functioning of your thyroid. Try checking your diet first. There are certain kinds of food that are not good for your thyroid health.

Try to familiarize yourself with recent studies that could give you the evidence you need regarding those types of food. A good example is gluten, as it is known to have a link to triggering your body to develop autoimmune diseases. Studies have indeed shown that having a gluten allergy or sensitivity can bring about a lot of symptoms, including weight gain and fatigue.

Pesticides have also been known to be bad for the thyroid. You have to make sure that you aid your body's own detoxification by taking necessary steps, such as drinking filtered water and eating organic and detoxifying food. Avoid fluoride and chlorinated water.

Chronic stress also affects the function of the thyroid. Make sure that you have various ways to de-stress yourself to avoid stressing your thyroid, too.

Get fit by doing regular exercise and going to saunas.

A lot of people don't know that exercise also stimulates the thyroid gland to work, and it also boosts the sensitivity of body tissues to the thyroid hormones. Steam baths or saunas also help the body to flush out any toxins taken from pesticides. Pesticides carry toxins that are detrimental to your thyroid, which is why you should detoxify yourself. You can choose to do yoga or any other form of exercise.

By going to the sauna, you are aiding your body to lose weight, as well as repair the thyroid. How is that possible? When you lose weight, fat tissues release toxins like organochlorines that are normally found in pesticides. These toxins have been found to lower the T3 levels, which then slows down your metabolic rate when at rest. Detoxification is an important process in order to improve the function of your thyroid.

Only eat the food that will support your thyroid nutritionally, and avoid the food that doesn't.

The Atkins Thyroid Diet depends on what you also eat. By eating the right food, you are helping your body, especially your thyroid to heal. You have to use the right food to send the right signals to your genes. The production of the thyroid hormones requires omega-3 fatty acids and iodine. Selenium is required to activate T4 to become T3. The binding of the hormone T3 to the nucleus' receptor requires zinc and vitamins D and A. You will be able to find all of these in a diet that is clean, whole-food, and organic.

Other foods that can help the thyroid to function normally include sea vegetables and seaweeds since they are rich in iodine. Fish, especially salmon and sardines, also contains iodine, Vitamin D, and omega-3 fats. Dark leafy greens, dandelion, and mustard have Vitamin A. Scallops, smelt, Brazil nuts, and herring have selenium in them.

Avoid foods that contain gluten. When it comes to soy products, it is important that you get only clean sources, and make sure that you only take these in moderation. Avoid those processed ones.

Take supplements that will help your thyroid.

The important elements for a healthy functioning thyroid include the intake of supplements. Be sure to take a multivitamin, as well as a mineral supplement that has omega-3 fats, iodine, vitamins A and D, plus zinc.

At the same time, if your adrenal glands have become subjected to long-term stresses, you also have to support them. Make sure to take supplements or herbs that are adaptogenic, such as ginseng and rhodiola. This will prevent your body from feeling ill. You can ask your doctor or general practitioner if they can help you focus on the needs of your thyroid, and if needed, your adrenal glands, too.

Get yourself tested, especially your thyroid.

There is no perfect way of knowing or diagnosing hypo-thyroidism or poor thyroid function. Having one symptom doesn't mean that you already are suffering from a thyroid condition. The important thing to do is to check both your blood tests and symptoms. Doctors would diagnose if you have a thyroid problem by checking the TSH levels in your body. Sometimes, they may also ask for a free T4 level test.

But a lot of health practitioners have questioned the "normal" levels if they really are to be considered normal. Be sure to find a doctor that is experienced in ordering and interpreting the results of your tests. They will be able to get a better understanding of your thyroid's health condition.

These are some strategies that you could follow in order to make sure that your thyroid will be functioning optimally again.

5 - Conclusion

Aside from a malfunctioning thyroid, there may also be other problems that could arise from having an unhealthy thyroid. It has been found that thyroid patients are gullible to some types of gut imbalances due to how the thyroid hormones act in the gut.

First of all, the thyroid hormone boosts intestinal peristalsis, a term used to describe the gut's natural movement. The hormone also aids the body in regulating the normal amount of stomach acid that is needed to break down the food that you eat.

When a person has problems with the thyroid, such as a sluggish one, he or she is bound to have gut imbalances. Some common imbalances found in people who have Hashimoto's disease or hypothyroidism include the following: yeast overgrowth, irritable bowel syndrome, small intestinal bacterial overgrowth, and Gastric-esophageal reflux (GERD). It is important that the imbalances of the gut are also treated beforehand so that your thyroid will also work perfectly.

It is therefore imperative that a person who suspects that he or she is suffering from hypothyroidism to also have a battery of tests conducted (as per order of his or her doctor). This is to check if there are other problems in the body that need to be addressed. This will ensure that not only the thyroid will be healthy, but the entire body, too.

Thank You

As we reach the end of this book, I want to say thanks for reading this book.

I want to get this information out to as many people as possible. If you found this book helpful, I would greatly appreciate you leaving me a review. This helps others find the book as well.

This book was self-published with the amazing help of Self-Publishing Made Easy Now! [3] . You can grab a free copy of the checklist that started my journey here: FREE Self-Publishing Checklist [4] .

[3] https://selfpublishingmadeeasynow.com/xpjv
[4] https://selfpublishingmadeeasynow.com/free_checklist

Disclaimer

This document is geared towards providing exact and reliable information in regards to the topic and issue covered. The publication is sold on the idea that the publisher is not required to render an accounting, officially permitted, or otherwise, qualified services. If advice is necessary, legal, financial, medical or professional, a practiced individual in the profession should be ordered.

This information is not presented by a financial or medical practitioner and is for entertainment, educational and informational purposes only. The content is not intended as a substitute for professional medical advice, diagnosis, or treatment.

Always seek the advice of your physician or other qualified health care provider with any questions you may have regarding a medical condition. Never disregard professional medical advice or delay in seeking it because of something you have read.

The information provided herein is stated to be truthful and consistent, in that any liability, in terms of inattention or otherwise, by any usage or abuse of any policies, processes, or directions contained within is the solitary and utter re-

DISCLAIMER

sponsibility of the recipient reader.

Under no circumstances will any legal responsibility or blame be held against the publisher for any reparation, damages, or monetary loss due to the information herein, either directly or indirectly.